Conrad K. Butler

Counting with Critters

1

One little duckling swims in the pond, all by itself, but very fond.

2

Two horses gallop across the field, racing together with great zeal.

Three sheep graze in
the meadow, one, two, three
– side by side, nice and
mellow.

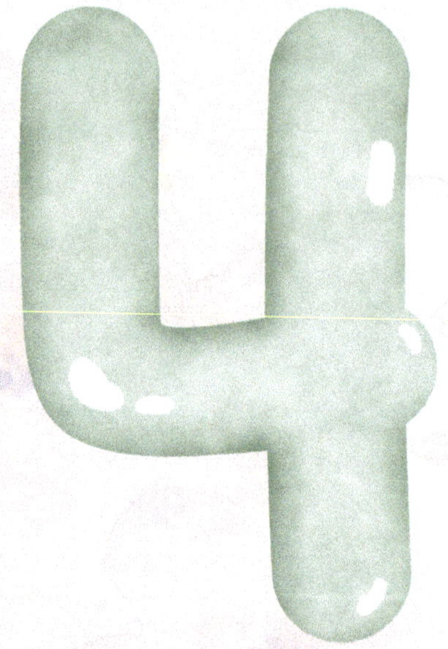

4

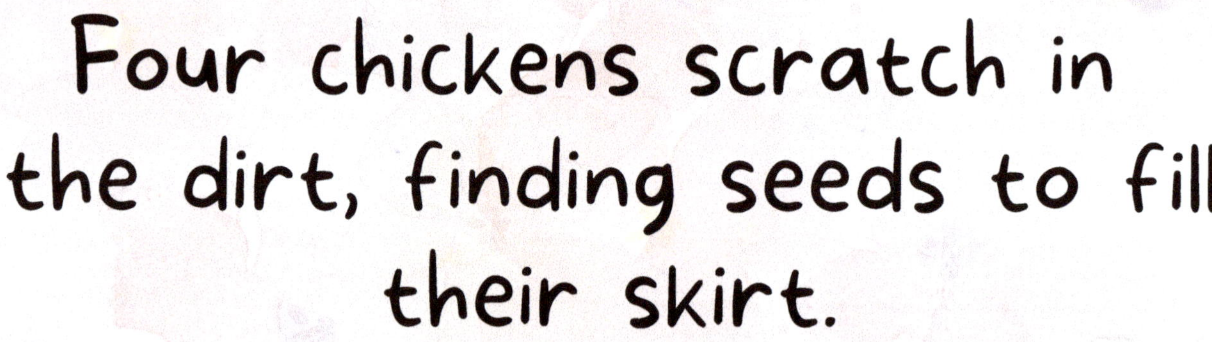

Four chickens scratch in
the dirt, finding seeds to fill
their skirt.

5

Five piglets rolling in the mud,
each one a happy little bud.

6

Six bunnies hopping on
the lawn, up and down
from dusk till dawn.

7

Seven bees buzzing near the flowers, gathering nectar for hours.

Eight frogs sitting by
the pond, croaking and
hopping, here and beyond.

9

Nine chicks follow their mother, all in a row, one after another.

Ten birds flying in the sky, soaring high as they wave goodbye.

Check also:

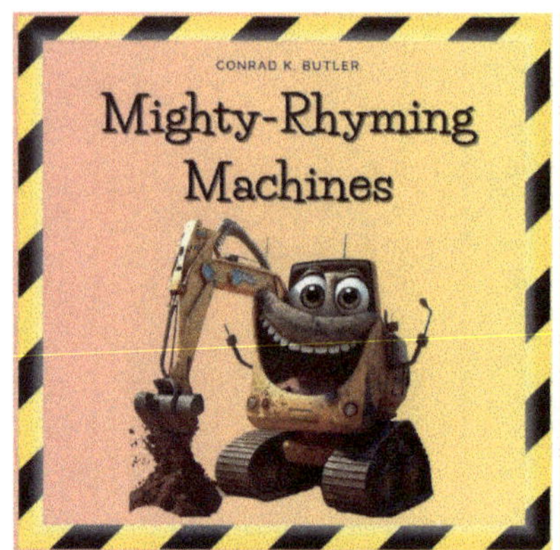

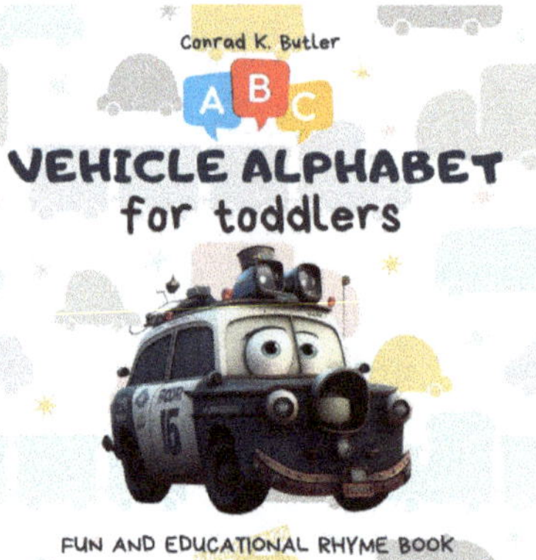

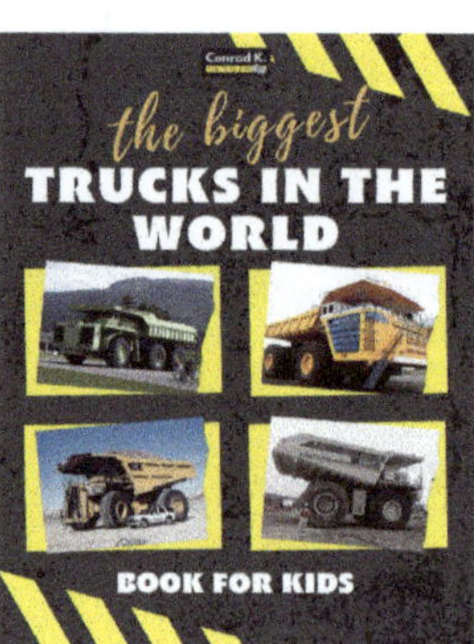

and much more!